• LEARNING HOW •
KARATE

BY
JANE MERSKY LEDER

597760

Bancroft-Sage Publishing

601 Elkcam Circle, Suite C-7, P. O. 355   Marco, Florida 33969-0355 USA

3361193

• LEARNING HOW •
KARATE

AUTHOR
JANE MERSKY LEDER

EDITED BY
JODY JAMES

DESIGNED BY
CONCEPT and DESIGN

PHOTO CREDITS

Alan Leder: Cover, Pages 4, 5, 15, 17, 19, 21, 22, 23, 24, 25, 26, 27, 28, 29, 30, 31, 32, 33, 34, 35, 36, 37, 38, 40, 42.
Unicorn Stock Photos: Dick Young - Pages 7, 39, 41, 48b;
Sue Vanderbilt - Pages 13, 45, 48a;
Tom McCarthy - Page 48c.

ACKNOWLEDGMENTS

Many thanks to Brian, Magdalena, Bardia, Lindsay, Max, Katie, Fortino, Ava, Andrew, Raquel, Eric, Jorge, Amy, Matthew, Juan, Kleber, Aaron, Josh and Craig. You were all terrific! And to Sensei Bambouyani, Marianne Hefferon, Nathan Gyven, and Bill Billings of the Japan Karate Association's central region main dojo in Chicago, Illinois—your expertise, time, and energy were invaluable.

TABLE OF CONTENTS

**LIBRARY OF CONGRESS
CATALOGING-IN-PUBLICATION DATA**

Leder, Jane Mersky.
  Learning how: karate / by Jane Mersky Leder; edited by Jody James; illustrated by Concept and Design.
    p.   cm. – (Learning how sports)
  Summary: Introduces the exciting sport of karate, describing its history, exercises, types of holds, safety factors, and competitions.
  ISBN 0-944280-34-X (lib. bdg.) – ISBN 0-944280-39-0 (pbk.)
    1. Karate – Juvenile literature. [1. Karate.]   I. Title.   II. Series
GV1114.3.L396   1992
796.8'153–dc20   91-23652
                                                                        CIP
                                                                        AC

International Standard Book Number:	**Library of Congress Catalog Card Number:**
Library Binding 0-944280-34-X Paperback Binding 0-944280-39-0	91-23652

INTRODUCTION

The two karate students face each other. They bow to each other as a sign of mutual respect. The **step-sparring** (controlled combat) is about to begin.

Karate students bow to each other at the beginning and the end of each step-sparring session.

The attacker drops back into an attacking position. The defender remains in her "ready" stance. The attacker announces his move. He is going to do a front kick. The defender acknowledges that she is ready. Then she drops back. As the attacker's leg reaches toward her, the defender uses the outer edge of her wrist and forearm to block the kick.

The attacker does four more moves. Before each move, he announces what he is going to do. Each time, he waits for his opponent to acknowledge that she is ready.

Step-sparring is a way to develop control and to practice self-defense skills with a partner. Each move is done slowly. Distance, timing, and focus are very important. An attacker must stand so that his or her punches and kicks stop within one inch of the opponent's body. The timing must be exact, and both students must concentrate. Both students must focus all of their energy on the exercise.

At the end of the step-sparring session, the two **karateka** (karate students) bow to each other again. They are tired but happy. Karate has helped them concentrate. It has made them stronger and more confident.

Step-sparring helps develop control and self-defense skills.

CHAPTER ONE:

Karate: Not Just Self-Defense

Karate is much more than a way to protect yourself. It is also a sport and even a way of life. As a sport, karate is exciting for both the players and the fans. It is a test of a person's fighting abilities that has built-in safeguards. All punches and kicks stop within an inch of the opponent's body. Poor conduct and dangerous actions are not allowed.

There are many ways to benefit from the sport of karate.

In karate tournaments, a **referee** stands on the competition floor. It is usually his or her job to call a point. A point is called when the referee feels that a punch or kick was done with enough skill and power to have hurt if it had struck the opponent. The referee often relies on one of the four corner judges to help call a point. At least one of the four judges is usually able to see a punch or kick clearly.

During a karate tournament, a referee stands on the competition floor to call earned points to the players.

Karate teaches important lessons that go far beyond the **dojo**, or karate school. For example, part of learning karate is learning to develop patience. Getting a punch or block right takes a lot of hard work. Therefore, the sport teaches discipline and concentration. Karate also boosts self-confidence and teaches that it is okay to make mistakes. Everyone does.

Karate is not just a sport of punches and kicks. It is a way to improve your mind, too. Good karateka do not think they are better than others. They control their negative feelings. They respect others and *their* feelings.

When karateka are asked about karate, they use words like *confidence, concentration*, and *strength*. They use words like *fun* and *exciting*, too. Karate has helped many students focus more on their schoolwork. In other cases, karate helps students control their temper.

Yes, karate prepares you to defend yourself, if that is ever necessary. But karate is also a way of life.

Karate teaches important lessons like patience and concentration.

The sensei, or instructor, helps a student with positioning, as he attempts a side thrust kick.

CHAPTER TWO:

The History of Karate

As the story is told, a Buddhist monk named Daruma walked from India to China 1500 years ago. His goal was to teach his religion to the Chinese monks. The Chinese found his teachings very hard. Daruma decided to add exercises to his teachings. That way, the monks could place the hard lessons between periods of physical exercise. The lessons might not seem so hard if they were broken into shorter time periods. The exercises would also help the monks develop their bodies as well as their minds.

As time went on, the exercises became a form of self-defense. Because of their religion, the monks could not use weapons. They practiced the self-defense exercises to protect themselves against thieves while they traveled around the countryside.

This form of self-defense began to spread to other countries, including the island of Okinawa. During the seventeenth century, the Japanese took over the island of Okinawa. They would not allow the Okinawans to practice any form of self-defense. The Okinawan men began working in secret on self-defense. They often worked in small caves. They developed their hands and feet into weapons.

The Okinawans secretly continued to practice self-defense at night. In the early 1900s, the self-defense was practiced more openly and was called **karate**. The word karate is Japanese for "empty hand." Several men became well known for their karate skills. These men became "masters." Many of the masters started their own karate systems. One of these men was Gichin Funakoshi. In 1922, Master Funakoshi was chosen to go to Japan to show the Japanese his karate.

The Japanese were very impressed. By 1932, all of the universities in Japan had karate dojos. Master Funakoshi became known as "the Father of Modern-Day Karate."

After World War II, many American servicemen and women began studying karate. They had been stationed in Japan during the war and had seen this exciting form of self-defense. It was not until the mid-1950s, however, that karate started becoming popular in America. By the 1970s, karate had become very popular. Bruce Lee movies were popular, and the *Kung Fu* series was being shown on television.

Today, karate remains a popular sport. Karate tournaments are shown on television. Movies such as *The Karate Kid* have sparked young people's interest in learning karate.

Karate has become a very popular sport in America. This photo shows a class in progress.

CHAPTER THREE:

Getting Started

There are many sports in which your size and sex determine whether or not you can play. If you are not very tall, chances are that you will not play on a basketball team. If you are not big and strong, you probably will not play football. If you are female, playing a game like football can be a real challenge.

Things are different in karate. You can be big or small. You can be male or female. You can be ten years old or forty years old. Karate is challenging and educational. But anyone who makes up his or her mind to stick with karate can enjoy the art and progress. Becoming a better karateka simply depends on the amount of time you spend practicing each week.

You do not need a big space in which to practice karate. You can use a room in your house or apartment. A basement or garage will do. Remember that many of the Okinawan men had to exercise in secret.

You do not need a lot of equipment to practice karate, either. You wear a uniform called a **gi**. A gi consists of a loose, comfortable pair of pants and a top. Karate students practice and spar in their bare feet. Besides your uniform, you might want to add a full-length mirror to a wall. You can use the mirror to make sure that your form is correct.

Karate is said to be one of the best forms of physical training. Karate students who train hard stay in very good physical shape. Karate also keeps students in top mental health, because it requires them to use both their bodies and their minds. It builds self-confidence that carries over into daily life.

Many karate instructors talk about the pleasure of teaching. They watch their students grow month by month. Some instructors say that many of their students are changed into new people!

Karate channels your energy in positive ways. You concentrate so hard on what you are doing that you forget any negative or angry feelings that you may bring with you to karate class.

This father and son perform Okinawan Karate. Notice the uniforms, or gi, that they wear.

Karate is not an easy sport. There will be times when you are ready to give up. Maybe your techniques do not seem to be improving. Or maybe your kicks are not getting any more direct. But do not give up. Every karate master has felt frustrated many times. Some instructors suggest that you set a goal before you try your first karate punch or kick. Keep that goal in your mind at all times. Setting a goal will help you get through the tough spots.

The Opening Ceremony

Respect is an important part of karate. Respect for the dojo, for the spirits of the karate masters, for the **sensei** (teacher), and for the other karateka are required. The opening ceremony, or program, is a way for everyone to clear their minds and to focus all of their energy on karate. It takes place before each karate class. This opening ceremony is one of the many Japanese traditions that connects karateka all over the world.

For the opening ceremony, the karateka line up according to belt order. The black belts are the most accomplished karateka. They stand on the far left. The brown belts stand next to them. Then come the purple, green, orange, yellow, and white belts. The sensei stands in front, facing the same direction as the students.

Everyone kneels on the sensei's instructions. They close their eyes and clear their minds of everything from outside the dojo. When told to do so, everyone opens their eyes. The karateka then bow with respect to the dojo and to the memory of the karate masters. The sensei turns around to face the karateka. Everyone bows to the sensei. The sensei then bows and stands up. Then, one by one, the karateka stand.

This student with closed eyes is meditating during the opening ceremony.

Everyone kneels for the opening ceremony. They close their eyes and clear their minds of everything outside the dojo.

Stretching

Karateka must warm up before they practice a single punch or kick. The best way to warm up is to do a series of stretching exercises. These exercises help make your body stronger and more flexible. The more flexible you are, the less chance you have of injuring yourself. Flexibility also helps you make beautiful kicks and be quick on your feet.

The stretching exercises for karate are designed to loosen the muscles from head to toe. Many students begin with head and neck turns. You can do shoulder shrugs, shrugging your shoulders forward, then backward. To loosen the muscles in the back and sides, you can twist your upper body to the left and to the right. To loosen the muscles of the waist and hips, you can do hip circles. (Imagine that you are trying to keep a hula hoop circling your waist as you move your hips in wide circles.)

To loosen the knees, you can do knee rotations. Then you can bend your upper body forward at the waist as far as it will go to loosen the muscles in your lower back and hamstrings. A good way to stretch the groin muscle is to bend one knee while keeping the other leg straight with the foot flat on the floor. Splits are another stretch to loosen the groin and inner thigh muscles. You may never be able to do a perfect split. That is not the idea. The point is to increase your flexibility a little bit at a time.

You should do these drills and others before every karate workout. You should never try to kick or punch without stretching first.

Stretching exercises are necessary to warm up before practicing a single punch or kick.

CHAPTER FOUR:

Kihon: The Basics

Kihon is the Japanese word for the basics of karate. Every karate student must learn the basics and practice them during every class. It does not matter what belt level a student has earned. He or she goes over the basics many times at the beginning of every class.

The basics of karate include form, technique, stance, and posture. As a karate student, you will work on each of these four areas. As you practice, you will develop good form. Your technique will become stronger. You will achieve proper balance and breathing.

The **stance**, or position of your legs and feet, is the basis for all parts of karate. The karate stance is designed to be perfectly balanced. When a karateka is standing in a perfectly balanced position, he or she can move in any direction. There are many karate stances. This book will explain two of them.

To find your stance, stand at attention with your feet together and your hands at your sides. Spread your feet to shoulder width. Then move the left foot ahead one step, and turn your body about 45 degrees to the right. (Your body will be halfway to the right.) Bend your left knee to cover your toes. Most of your weight should be on your left front foot, with the front toes pointing slightly inward and with the toes on your back foot facing forward as much as possible. You are now in what is called the **front stance**. From this stance, you can do any of the karate techniques.

The stance is the basis for all parts of karate. This student is practicing the front stance.

While in the front stance, keep your knees bent and your body low.

To move forward in the front stance, move your right foot close to your left foot. Step forward so that your left foot is the same distance from the standing leg as it was before you moved. To do the front stance with your left foot forward, repeat the same moves with your left side.

Once you are in the front stance, keep your knees bent and your body low. This helps you move without telegraphing (giving away your next move).

In the **back stance**, the toes on your back foot are turned in slightly. Most of your weight is on your back foot. The heels of your feet are in line with each other. Your back knee covers the toes on the back foot. In this stance, your hips are tucked under. Your hips should be at a 45-degree angle to the front facing sideways to your opponent. Both of your knees are pressed out.

This student is working on his back stance.

The Punches

As a beginner, you will learn basic karate punches. The karate punches are strong, but it is correct technique that makes them effective. The basic karate punches are done with a closed fist. To make a proper fist, hold the punching hand with the fingers pointing straight up. Then bend all the fingers tightly and tuck the thumb over the two knuckles nearest the thumb. These knuckles make up the striking area that is aimed at an opponent's face, and solar plexus (the hollow below the lower end of the breastbone), or lower section of the body.

Any punch can be done with either the right hand or the left hand. In this book, we will describe how to do each punch with the right hand.

The basic karate punches are done with a closed fist, making sure the thumb and fingers are in the proper position.

The **straight punch**, or **front punch**, begins with the right fist clenched, palm up, just above the right hip. Your left hand is open in front of the solar plexus. You pull your left elbow back at the same time and punch with your right fist. Make sure that your right forearm scrapes against the side of your body and then punches straight out. Just before the point of contact, turn your right wrist so that the palm is facing toward the floor.

As you punch straight out, you flick your right hip. It is the rapid thrusting of the right hip that swings the arm forward and gives the punch its power. All punches get their strength from the lower center of the body, not just from the movement of the arm.

This student has just completed a front punch with arm out and palm facing toward the floor.

You can do a **reverse punch** from a front stance after you have stepped forward and done a block (to be discussed in the next section) to protect yourself from an opponent's attack. To do a reverse punch, you use the force and weight of your entire body as it rapidly moves from a 45-degree angle to a 90-degree angle. (In a 90-degree angle, your chest is facing your opponent.) Again, it is the force of the center of your body that gives the punch its power. While you twist your hips to a 90-degree angle, you use your free hand to throw a reverse punch to the exposed body part of your opponent.

A reverse punch from the front stance uses the force and weight of your entire body.

A **lunge punch** begins from the front stance. As you move forward into the low, deep front stance, you do a straight, or front, punch. If your right leg is forward, you punch with your right fist. If your left leg is forward, you punch with your left fist.

There are more hand techniques that you will learn as you develop your karate skills. For now, practice these basic punches over and over again. You can never practice a karate punch too much or too often.

The lunge punch is delivered with the left leg and the left fist in the forward position.

The Blocks

For every punch, there is a **block**. A block stops an opponent's punch. It also allows you to counterattack.

As a beginning karate student, you will learn four basic blocks. A **rising block** blocks a punch to the face. With your right fist facing up and resting on your right hip, raise your right arm in a bent position above your head. This upward motion deflects an opponent's punch to the face. Your left hand is ready to throw a counterpunch.

The rising block blocks a punch to the face.

This student is completing a rising block. The upward motion of the arm deflects an opponent's punch.

This student shows the first posture for an inward block.

The **inward block** is used to block a punch to the solar plexus. Your clenched fist is at shoulder level with the palm facing toward you. Your elbow is about the width of a fist away from your ribs. As you do the block, your fist comes from your ear into the center of your body. Your hips are at a 45-degree angle to your opponent.

The **outward block** also blocks a punch to the solar plexus. This block begins with the fist under the opposite armpit, with the elbow bent. You bring the fist out quickly at shoulder level, so that the position is the same as for the inward block. The outward block catches the opponent's arm and deflects it to the side. Now the opponent's body is unprotected, and you can do a reverse punch.

This student shows the first posture for an outward block.

Completing posture for the outward block.

The **downward block** blocks an attack to the lower body. Your body is at a 90-degree angle to your opponent. Your left hand is in a fist, and your left arm is straight out at waist level. Your right fist is clenched at your left ear. As you pull your left arm back to your left hip, you scrape your right arm down the length of your left arm until it is almost fully extended, one fist's width above the right knee. At this point, you are in a 45-degree front stance. Your right fist will deflect a kick or punch to the outside of your body. Then you can do a counterattack.

Demonstrated in this photo is the first posture of a downward block. Your left hand is in a fist, and your left arm is straight out at waist level.

This photo shows the next posture of a downward block. As you pull your left arm back to your left hip, you scrape your right arm down the length of your left arm, until fully extended.

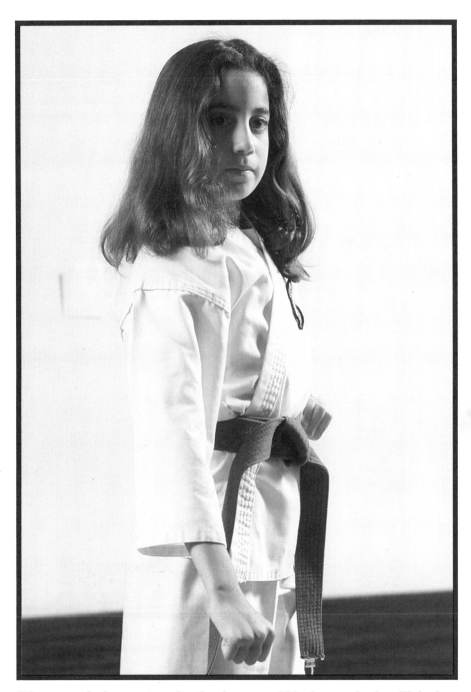

**When completing posture for the downward block, your body will be in a
45-degree front stance, ready to counterattack.**

Kicks

The powerful kicks are very important in karate. The legs are longer and stronger than the arms. When you add kicks to your arsenal, you double your ability to defend yourself against an opponent. A kick can be done with either foot. There are many karate kicks, but this book will concentrate on the three basic ones.

A good way to learn all of the karate kicks is to do them in slow motion. To execute a **front kick**, begin with your feet together and your knees bent. The striking area for the front kick is the ball of the foot. Scrape your right foot up along the inside of your left leg. Point your knee and foot toward the target. Next, snap your lower right leg out and back. The snap is quick and hard. As you snap the leg, the pelvis

This student demonstrates the first posture of a front kick. With feet together and knees bent, scrape your right foot up along the inside of your left leg.

thrusts slightly forward. It is this thrust that gives the kick its power. To complete the front kick, you scrape your right foot down the inside of the left leg and back to the original position. This move can be used offensively or defensively.

This photo shows the next posture of a front kick. Snap your lower right leg out and back. The snap is quick and hard.

Another basic kick in karate is the **side snap kick**. You begin with your feet together and your knees bent. Bring your right leg up the inside of the left leg. The right knee should point out to the side, and the upper body should face the direction of the kick. Thrust the right hip to the right as the right leg and foot snap out to the side and back. Once again, your right foot rests against the inside of the left thigh. Then your right foot scrapes back down the inside of the left leg onto the floor.

The **side thrust kick** begins in the same way as the side snap kick. You thrust the leg out to the side and hold it there for a fraction of a second. Whether you use the right foot or the left foot, it has to be at a right angle to the leg. That way, you kick with the outside edge of the foot. After you have thrust your leg out to the side and held it there briefly, pull it back and scrape it down the inside of the opposite thigh and leg.

This student demonstrates the first posture of a side thrust kick. With feet together and knees bent, bring the right leg up the inside of the left leg.

This photo shows the completing posture of the side thrust kick. With leg thrust out to the side and held there briefly, pull it back and scrape it down the inside of the opposite thigh and leg.

Kumite: Step-Sparring

Kumite is the Japanese word for step-sparring. Step-sparring gives karate students the chance to practice the basic punches, blocks, and kicks with a classmate as a partner.

To begin kumite, your instructor will ask you to get a partner. The instructor will then tell you what karate moves to do and how many times to practice each move. For example, the instructor might ask you to execute a straight punch three times to the face. He or she may instruct your partner to use a rising block to block the punch each time. At no time do you make actual contact with your partner.

Whenever you step-spar, you begin and end with a bow for concentration, control, and respect. You must announce to your partner the move you are about to make. Your partner, in turn, must acknowledge that he or she has understood your intention.

Kumite or step-sparring gives karate students a chance to practice their moves with help from their instructor.

36

During kumite, you do the moves slowly. Your instructor or an advanced student will watch and correct any mistakes. At the end of kumite, you will have the chance to counterpunch. Your opponent will punch. You will block that punch and then throw a punch to the closest unprotected legal part of your opponent's body.

Kumite is the time to practice the application of the basic karate moves. It is an exciting part of each karate class. You and your partner will begin to understand how all of the separate karate moves work together.

Kumite is an exciting part of each karate class and will help you and your partner to understand how all of the different karate moves work together.

Kata: Form

Kata is an arranged set of movements that are made up from the basics of karate. Each movement is designed either to block or to attack an imaginary opponent. Each kata begins with a block, because karate is a way to defend yourself. Karate is never to be used offensively. As a karateka, you never begin a conflict.

To learn a kata, you start out very slowly, with the instructor correcting you along the way. When you have mastered a kata, you are ready to be tested. If you pass the test, you earn a karate belt. The higher the karate belt, the more advanced the katas become.

When you do a kata, you start and end at the same spot. Each kata has a specific number of moves that never change. Proper breathing, rhythm, and focus are all very important.

You start out very slowly with your instructor to learn a kata.

Even people who have earned the highest karate belts continue to practice the beginning katas. The goal of karate is to seek perfection. The key to becoming a good karateka is to practice over and over again. That is why it is not unusual to see black belts practicing with white belts in the same class.

The goal of karate is to seek perfection, that is why constant practice is so important.

Testing

Certain days are set aside as test days. On those days, karateka have the opportunity to earn karate belts. Each karateka must demonstrate a certain level of skill as his or her progress in kata, kumite, and certain basic skills is evaluated. The proper attitude and a strong spirit are also important.

The first belt a karateka can earn is a white belt. Typically, the next belt is a yellow belt. Then come an orange belt, a green belt, two levels of purple belts, three levels of brown belts, and ten levels of black belts. The belt colors may vary according to different karate organizations.

On testing days, students have the opportunity to earn karate belts. Each color of belt represents a different level of skill.

CHAPTER FIVE:

Competition

Karateka can enter karate competitions at the local, state, regional, and national levels. Competitions are fun and challenging. Karateka compete as individuals and as a team. The categories of competition include kata and kumite. The goal is for each karateka to do his or her personal best.

The main dojo in the Japan Karate Association's central region is in Chicago, Illinois. Karateka from this dojo participated in a national tournament that was held in Denver, Colorado. The event drew competitors from nine regions, including Alaska and Florida. Individual and team competitions were held in kata and kumite.

These karate students exchange kicks at a national tournament held in Denver, Colorado.

The competitive divisions included children ages 7 to 9, male and female youth between the ages of 10 and 13, male and female open, and a "senior" division for karateka over the age of 40.

The preliminary competitions consisted of five competitions that were held at the same time. Those karateka who won the preliminaries went on to the finals. The finals began with a procession, with each region carrying its own banner. The national anthems of both Japan and the United States were played. Then the final competitions began.

All of the weeks, months, and years of training paid off. When it was all over, the Chicago karateka had done very well. Sensei Bambouyani told his students after the competition, "We will have to work hard to maintain our high standards and to repeat this success next year."

Competition can be fun and challenging. You have to practice all the time to maintain high levels of skill.

Competition Seen Through the Eyes of a Karateka

One member of the Chicago team recorded her feelings about a regional competition weekend. As a "lower belt," she was "in awe of this art (karate), and how much it entails." She continued, "A couple of 'higher belts' tell me that this is their first competition, too. They say they are also nervous. There are a few little girls competing, but I don't really notice how well they are doing because I am struck by how beautiful they are.

"My turn. I stand in the center of the five judges. This feels so strange! A kata is named, and I begin. When it is over and I am standing on the sideline once more, I have no idea how I did. I cannot remember my score.

"I realize that the differences here do not reflect age, race, sex, or creed, but spirit and knowledge.

"Awards are distributed, and each person receives a medal or a trophy—nice mementos of a great weekend. Everyone has had fun, and the children have impressed me with their sense of sportsmanship.

"The pre-examination workout is held the next morning, and it is hard. Sensei repeatedly switches the black belts who are helping the different groups, and each one finds something different that we are doing wrong! And they are all correct. We feel as though we know nothing.

"There must be 40 people to be tested. Much of the next two-and-a-half hours are but a blur for me. Three of us stand before the judges to perform kata. I exhale with each move, yet find myself out of breath by the time I finish. What seems like a year passes, while we stand at attention. Finally, we are dismissed, and someone whispers, 'Well, that was just as nerve-racking as I though it would be!'

"Two young yellow belts, who are the same size and who have trained together, perform their kata. One is blond, and the other is dark. They move as one, and the audience is obviously pleased with the visual effect this duo creates.

"Now it is over, and we must await the judges' decisions.

"Sensei gives a talk on dojo standards. Failure to earn a promotion means more work. However, because he does not intend to give up on us, we should not give up on ourselves.

"Most people pass. Three white belts earn double promotions, and they are stunned. A few children must train for another month. It is hard to watch their faces, and I think to myself, 'A month is not long.' But I am not one of those children.

"My name is called. I have passed!

"On the way home, I think about what the weekend has meant for me. I met new people and got to know others better. I have a new appreciation for the upper belts. Though I have felt the stress of competition and the fear of failure, I know there is no room for ego and that at no time was I ever alone."

CONCLUSION

Karate instructors agree that the basics of karate are the most important part of karate education. They also agree that the key to excellence is repetition. If you want to be a good kicker, you must practice karate kicks over and over again. If you want to be a good puncher and blocker, you must practice those moves over and over again. You can never practice too much as a student of karate.

The purpose of karate is to improve the body and the mind. It is important to have the proper mental attitude when you study karate. Advanced karateka can learn more by helping each other. When you go to a karate class, you should practice to improve yourself and to help others improve.

Karate takes time. Practice as often as possible. Listen carefully to your instructors. Watch your instructors and other senior students. Ask questions. Most of all, enjoy the many ways in which you benefit from karate!

The purpose of karate is to improve the body and the mind. Listen carefully to your instructors.

GLOSSARY

back stance - stance in which most of your weight is on your back foot, with your heels in a line, your back knee covering the toes on the back foot, your hips tucked under, and your knees pressed out

block - a karate move that blocks an opponent's punch or kick

dojo - a karate school

downward block - a block to deflect an opponent's front kick or low attack

front kick - a hard, quick snap kick, with the knee and foot pointed toward the target

front punch - see *straight punch*

front stance - a stance from which you punch or block punches and kicks; in this stance, most of your weight is on your front foot, with the toes on your back foot facing forward as much as possible and the toes on the front foot pointing slightly inward

gi - a karate uniform

inward block - a block that deflects an opponent's punch to the solar plexus

karate - the Japanese word that means "empty hand"

karateka - a karate student

kata - the Japanese word for "form"; a series of arranged movements that begins with a block and is done with four or more imaginary attackers

kihon - the basic karate skills, which include form, technique, stance, and posture

kumite - step-sparring, in which karateka practice karate skills with a partner

lunge punch - a punch that is done as you move into a front stance, with the same foot and hand forward

outward block - a move that blocks an opponent's punch to the solar plexus

referee - an official who awards points at a karate competition

reverse punch - a punch done after a block in which you twist your hips to a 90° angle and use your free hand to throw a punch to the exposed body part of your opponent

rising block - a move that blocks an opponent's attack to the face

sensei - the Japanese word for "teacher"

side snap kick - a kick in which the leg snaps out to the side and back

side thrust kick - a side kick in which you thrust the leg to the side

stance - the position of your legs and feet in karate

step-sparring - see *kumite*

straight punch - a punch in which the fist and forearm punch straight out; just before contact, the wrist of the punching hand is turned over so that the palm is toward the floor